Don't Be Feeling Blue

A Blue Colored Password Journal

Activinotes

Activinotes

DAILY JOURNALS, PLANNERS, NOTEBOOKS AND OTHER BLANK BOOKS

Copyright 2016

Password Journal

Notes :

Account Name: _____

Website : _____

User I.D. : _____

Email Used : _____

Password : _____

Account Name: _____

Website : _____

User I.D. : _____

Email Used : _____

Password : _____

Notes :

Notes :

Account Name: _____

Website : _____

User I.D. : _____

Email Used : _____

Password : _____

Account Name: _____

Website : _____

User I.D. : _____

Email Used : _____

Password : _____

Notes :

Don't be feeling blue

Don't be feeling blue

Password Journal

Notes :

Account Name: _____

Website : _____

User I.D. : _____

Email Used : _____

Password : _____

Account Name: _____

Website : _____

User I.D. : _____

Email Used : _____

Password : _____

Notes :

Notes :

Account Name: _____

Website : _____

User I.D. : _____

Email Used : _____

Password : _____

Account Name: _____

Website : _____

User I.D. : _____

Email Used : _____

Password : _____

Notes :

Don't be feeling blue

Smile

Don't be feeling blue

Password Journal

Notes :

Account Name: _____

Website : _____

User I.D. : _____

Email Used : _____

Password : _____

Account Name: _____

Website : _____

User I.D. : _____

Email Used : _____

Password : _____

Notes :

Notes :

Account Name: _____

Website : _____

User I.D. : _____

Email Used : _____

Password : _____

Account Name: _____

Website : _____

User I.D. : _____

Email Used : _____

Password : _____

Notes :

Don't be feeling blue

Don't be feeling blue

Smile

Password Journal

Notes :

Account Name: _____

Website : _____

User I.D. : _____

Email Used : _____

Password : _____

Account Name: _____

Website : _____

User I.D. : _____

Email Used : _____

Password : _____

Notes :

Notes :

Account Name: _____

Website : _____

User I.D. : _____

Email Used : _____

Password : _____

Account Name: _____

Website : _____

User I.D. : _____

Email Used : _____

Password : _____

Notes :

Don't be feeling blue

Smile

Don't be feeling blue

Password Journal

Notes :

Account Name: _____

Website : _____

User I.D. : _____

Email Used : _____

Password : _____

Account Name: _____

Website : _____

User I.D. : _____

Email Used : _____

Password : _____

Notes :

Notes :

Account Name: _____

Website : _____

User I.D. : _____

Email Used : _____

Password : _____

Account Name: _____

Website : _____

User I.D. : _____

Email Used : _____

Password : _____

Notes :

Don't be feeling blue

Password Journal

Don't be feeling blue

Smile

Password Journal

Notes :

Account Name: _____

Website : _____

User I.D. : _____

Email Used : _____

Password : _____

Account Name: _____

Website : _____

User I.D. : _____

Email Used : _____

Password : _____

Notes :

Notes :

Account Name: _____

Website : _____

User I.D. : _____

Email Used : _____

Password : _____

Account Name: _____

Website : _____

User I.D. : _____

Email Used : _____

Password : _____

Notes :

Don't be feeling blue

Don't be feeling blue

Password Journal

Notes :

Account Name: _____

Website : _____

User I.D. : _____

Email Used : _____

Password : _____

Account Name: _____

Website : _____

User I.D. : _____

Email Used : _____

Password : _____

Notes :

Notes :

Account Name: _____

Website : _____

User I.D. : _____

Email Used : _____

Password : _____

Account Name: _____

Website : _____

User I.D. : _____

Email Used : _____

Password : _____

Notes :

Don't be feeling blue

Smile

Don't be feeling blue

Password Journal

Notes :

Account Name: _____

Website : _____

User I.D. : _____

Email Used : _____

Password : _____

Account Name: _____

Website : _____

User I.D. : _____

Email Used : _____

Password : _____

Notes :

Notes :

Account Name: _____

Website : _____

User I.D. : _____

Email Used : _____

Password : _____

Account Name: _____

Website : _____

User I.D. : _____

Email Used : _____

Password : _____

Notes :

Don't be feeling blue

Smile

Don't be feeling blue

Password Journal

Notes :

Account Name: _____

Website : _____

User I.D. : _____

Email Used : _____

Password : _____

Account Name: _____

Website : _____

User I.D. : _____

Email Used : _____

Password : _____

Notes :

Notes :

Account Name: _____

Website : _____

User I.D. : _____

Email Used : _____

Password : _____

Account Name: _____

Website : _____

User I.D. : _____

Email Used : _____

Password : _____

Notes :

Don't be feeling blue

Smile

Don't be feeling blue

Password Journal

Notes :

Account Name: _____

Website : _____

User I.D. : _____

Email Used : _____

Password : _____

Account Name: _____

Website : _____

User I.D. : _____

Email Used : _____

Password : _____

Notes :

Notes :

Account Name: _____

Website : _____

User I.D. : _____

Email Used : _____

Password : _____

Account Name: _____

Website : _____

User I.D. : _____

Email Used : _____

Password : _____

Notes :

Don't be feeling blue

Smile

Don't be feeling blue

Password Journal

Notes :

Account Name: _____

Website : _____

User I.D. : _____

Email Used : _____

Password : _____

Account Name: _____

Website : _____

User I.D. : _____

Email Used : _____

Password : _____

Notes :

Notes :

Account Name: _____

Website : _____

User I.D. : _____

Email Used : _____

Password : _____

Account Name: _____

Website : _____

User I.D. : _____

Email Used : _____

Password : _____

Notes :

Don't be feeling blue

Smile

Don't be feeling blue

Password Journal

Notes :

Account Name: _____

Website : _____

User I.D. : _____

Email Used : _____

Password : _____

Account Name: _____

Website : _____

User I.D. : _____

Email Used : _____

Password : _____

Notes :

Notes :

Account Name: _____

Website : _____

User I.D. : _____

Email Used : _____

Password : _____

Account Name: _____

Website : _____

User I.D. : _____

Email Used : _____

Password : _____

Notes :

Don't be feeling blue

Smile

Don't be feeling blue

Password Journal

Notes :

Account Name: _____

Website : _____

User I.D. : _____

Email Used : _____

Password : _____

Account Name: _____

Website : _____

User I.D. : _____

Email Used : _____

Password : _____

Notes :

Notes :

Account Name: _____

Website : _____

User I.D. : _____

Email Used : _____

Password : _____

Account Name: _____

Website : _____

User I.D. : _____

Email Used : _____

Password : _____

Notes :

Don't be feeling blue

Don't be feeling blue

Smile

Password Journal

Notes :

Account Name: _____

Website : _____

User I.D. : _____

Email Used : _____

Password : _____

Account Name: _____

Website : _____

User I.D. : _____

Email Used : _____

Password : _____

Notes :

Notes :

Account Name: _____

Website : _____

User I.D. : _____

Email Used : _____

Password : _____

Account Name: _____

Website : _____

User I.D. : _____

Email Used : _____

Password : _____

Notes :

Don't be feeling blue

Smile

Don't be feeling blue

Password Journal

Notes :

Account Name: _____

Website : _____

User I.D. : _____

Email Used : _____

Password : _____

Account Name: _____

Website : _____

User I.D. : _____

Email Used : _____

Password : _____

Notes :

Account Name: _____

Website : _____

User I.D. : _____

Email Used : _____

Password : _____

Notes :

Account Name: _____

Website : _____

User I.D. : _____

Email Used : _____

Password : _____

Notes :

Don't be feeling blue

Password Journal

Smile

Don't be feeling blue

Password Journal

Notes :

Account Name: _____

Website : _____

User I.D. : _____

Email Used : _____

Password : _____

Account Name: _____

Website : _____

User I.D. : _____

Email Used : _____

Password : _____

Notes :

Notes :

Account Name: _____

Website : _____

User I.D. : _____

Email Used : _____

Password : _____

Account Name: _____

Website : _____

User I.D. : _____

Email Used : _____

Password : _____

Notes :

Don't be feeling blue

Smile

Don't be feeling blue

Password Journal

Notes :

Account Name: _____

Website : _____

User I.D. : _____

Email Used : _____

Password : _____

Account Name: _____

Website : _____

User I.D. : _____

Email Used : _____

Password : _____

Notes :

Notes :

Account Name: _____

Website : _____

User I.D. : _____

Email Used : _____

Password : _____

Account Name: _____

Website : _____

User I.D. : _____

Email Used : _____

Password : _____

Notes :

Don't be feeling blue

Smile

Don't be feeling blue

Password Journal

Notes :

Account Name: _____
Website : _____
User I.D. : _____
Email Used : _____
Password : _____

Account Name: _____
Website : _____
User I.D. : _____
Email Used : _____
Password : _____

Notes :

Notes :

Account Name: _____
Website : _____
User I.D. : _____
Email Used : _____
Password : _____

Account Name: _____
Website : _____
User I.D. : _____
Email Used : _____
Password : _____

Notes :

Don't be feeling blue

Smile

Don't be feeling blue

Password Journal

Notes :

Account Name: _____

Website : _____

User I.D. : _____

Email Used : _____

Password : _____

Account Name: _____

Website : _____

User I.D. : _____

Email Used : _____

Password : _____

Notes :

Notes :

Account Name: _____

Website : _____

User I.D. : _____

Email Used : _____

Password : _____

Account Name: _____

Website : _____

User I.D. : _____

Email Used : _____

Password : _____

Notes :

Don't be feeling blue

Don't be feeling blue

Password Journal

Notes :

Account Name: _____

Website : _____

User I.D. : _____

Email Used : _____

Password : _____

Account Name: _____

Website : _____

User I.D. : _____

Email Used : _____

Password : _____

Notes :

Notes :

Account Name: _____

Website : _____

User I.D. : _____

Email Used : _____

Password : _____

Account Name: _____

Website : _____

User I.D. : _____

Email Used : _____

Password : _____

Notes :

Don't be feeling blue

Smile

Don't be feeling blue

Password Journal

Notes :

Account Name: _____

Website : _____

User I.D. : _____

Email Used : _____

Password : _____

Account Name: _____

Website : _____

User I.D. : _____

Email Used : _____

Password : _____

Notes :

Notes :

Account Name: _____

Website : _____

User I.D. : _____

Email Used : _____

Password : _____

Notes :

Account Name: _____

Website : _____

User I.D. : _____

Email Used : _____

Password : _____

Notes :

Don't be feeling blue

Smile

Don't be feeling blue

Password Journal

Notes :

Account Name: _____

Website : _____

User I.D. : _____

Email Used : _____

Password : _____

Account Name: _____

Website : _____

User I.D. : _____

Email Used : _____

Password : _____

Notes :

Notes :

Account Name: _____

Website : _____

User I.D. : _____

Email Used : _____

Password : _____

Account Name: _____

Website : _____

User I.D. : _____

Email Used : _____

Password : _____

Notes :

Don't be feeling blue

Smile

Don't be feeling blue

Password Journal

Notes :

Account Name: _____

Website : _____

User I.D. : _____

Email Used : _____

Password : _____

Account Name: _____

Website : _____

User I.D. : _____

Email Used : _____

Password : _____

Notes :

Notes :

Account Name: _____

Website : _____

User I.D. : _____

Email Used : _____

Password : _____

Account Name: _____

Website : _____

User I.D. : _____

Email Used : _____

Password : _____

Notes :

Don't be feeling blue

Don't be feeling blue

Password Journal

Notes :

Account Name: _____

Website : _____

User I.D. : _____

Email Used : _____

Password : _____

Account Name: _____

Website : _____

User I.D. : _____

Email Used : _____

Password : _____

Notes :

Notes :

Account Name: _____

Website : _____

User I.D. : _____

Email Used : _____

Password : _____

Account Name: _____

Website : _____

User I.D. : _____

Email Used : _____

Password : _____

Notes :

Don't be feeling blue

Smile

Don't be feeling blue

Password Journal

Notes :

Account Name: _____

Website : _____

User I.D. : _____

Email Used : _____

Password : _____

Account Name: _____

Website : _____

User I.D. : _____

Email Used : _____

Password : _____

Notes :

Notes :

Account Name: _____

Website : _____

User I.D. : _____

Email Used : _____

Password : _____

Account Name: _____

Website : _____

User I.D. : _____

Email Used : _____

Password : _____

Notes :

Don't be feeling blue

Smile

Don't be feeling blue

Password Journal

Notes :

Account Name: _____

Website : _____

User I.D. : _____

Email Used : _____

Password : _____

Account Name: _____

Website : _____

User I.D. : _____

Email Used : _____

Password : _____

Notes :

Notes :

Account Name: _____

Website : _____

User I.D. : _____

Email Used : _____

Password : _____

Account Name: _____

Website : _____

User I.D. : _____

Email Used : _____

Password : _____

Notes :

Don't be feeling blue

Smile

Don't be feeling blue

Password Journal

Notes :

Account Name: _____

Website : _____

User I.D. : _____

Email Used : _____

Password : _____

Account Name: _____

Website : _____

User I.D. : _____

Email Used : _____

Password : _____

Notes :

Notes :

Account Name: _____

Website : _____

User I.D. : _____

Email Used : _____

Password : _____

Account Name: _____

Website : _____

User I.D. : _____

Email Used : _____

Password : _____

Notes :

Don't be feeling blue

Don't be feeling blue

Password Journal

Notes :

Account Name: _____

Website : _____

User I.D. : _____

Email Used : _____

Password : _____

Account Name: _____

Website : _____

User I.D. : _____

Email Used : _____

Password : _____

Notes :

Notes :

Account Name: _____

Website : _____

User I.D. : _____

Email Used : _____

Password : _____

Account Name: _____

Website : _____

User I.D. : _____

Email Used : _____

Password : _____

Notes :

Don't be feeling blue

Smile

Don't be feeling blue

Password Journal

Notes :

Account Name: _____
Website : _____
User I.D. : _____
Email Used : _____
Password : _____

Account Name: _____
Website : _____
User I.D. : _____
Email Used : _____
Password : _____

Notes :

Notes :

Account Name: _____
Website : _____
User I.D. : _____
Email Used : _____
Password : _____

Account Name: _____
Website : _____
User I.D. : _____
Email Used : _____
Password : _____

Notes :

Don't be feeling blue

Smile

Don't be feeling blue

Password Journal

Notes :

Account Name: _____

Website : _____

User I.D. : _____

Email Used : _____

Password : _____

Account Name: _____

Website : _____

User I.D. : _____

Email Used : _____

Password : _____

Notes :

Notes :

Account Name: _____

Website : _____

User I.D. : _____

Email Used : _____

Password : _____

Account Name: _____

Website : _____

User I.D. : _____

Email Used : _____

Password : _____

Notes :

Don't be feeling blue

Don't be feeling blue

Password Journal

Notes :

Account Name: _____

Website : _____

User I.D. : _____

Email Used : _____

Password : _____

Account Name: _____

Website : _____

User I.D. : _____

Email Used : _____

Password : _____

Notes :

Notes :

Account Name: _____

Website : _____

User I.D. : _____

Email Used : _____

Password : _____

Account Name: _____

Website : _____

User I.D. : _____

Email Used : _____

Password : _____

Notes :

Don't be feeling blue

Smile

Don't be feeling blue

Password Journal

Notes :

Account Name: _____

Website : _____

User I.D. : _____

Email Used : _____

Password : _____

Account Name: _____

Website : _____

User I.D. : _____

Email Used : _____

Password : _____

Notes :

Notes :

Account Name: _____

Website : _____

User I.D. : _____

Email Used : _____

Password : _____

Account Name: _____

Website : _____

User I.D. : _____

Email Used : _____

Password : _____

Notes :

Don't be feeling blue

Smile

Don't be feeling blue

Password Journal

Notes :

Account Name: _____

Website : _____

User I.D. : _____

Email Used : _____

Password : _____

Account Name: _____

Website : _____

User I.D. : _____

Email Used : _____

Password : _____

Notes :

Notes :

Account Name: _____

Website : _____

User I.D. : _____

Email Used : _____

Password : _____

Account Name: _____

Website : _____

User I.D. : _____

Email Used : _____

Password : _____

Notes :

Don't be feeling blue

Don't be feeling blue

Password Journal

Notes :

Account Name: _____

Website : _____

User I.D. : _____

Email Used : _____

Password : _____

Account Name: _____

Website : _____

User I.D. : _____

Email Used : _____

Password : _____

Notes :

Notes :

Account Name: _____

Website : _____

User I.D. : _____

Email Used : _____

Password : _____

Account Name: _____

Website : _____

User I.D. : _____

Email Used : _____

Password : _____

Notes :

Don't be feeling blue

Smile

Don't be feeling blue

Password Journal

Notes :

Account Name: _____

Website : _____

User I.D. : _____

Email Used : _____

Password : _____

Account Name: _____

Website : _____

User I.D. : _____

Email Used : _____

Password : _____

Notes :

Notes :

Account Name: _____

Website : _____

User I.D. : _____

Email Used : _____

Password : _____

Account Name: _____

Website : _____

User I.D. : _____

Email Used : _____

Password : _____

Notes :

Don't be feeling blue

Smile

Don't be feeling blue

Password Journal

Notes :

Account Name: _____

Website : _____

User I.D. : _____

Email Used : _____

Password : _____

Account Name: _____

Website : _____

User I.D. : _____

Email Used : _____

Password : _____

Notes :

Notes :

Account Name: _____

Website : _____

User I.D. : _____

Email Used : _____

Password : _____

Account Name: _____

Website : _____

User I.D. : _____

Email Used : _____

Password : _____

Notes :

Don't be feeling blue

Smile

Don't be feeling blue

Password Journal

Notes :

Account Name: _____

Website : _____

User I.D. : _____

Email Used : _____

Password : _____

Account Name: _____

Website : _____

User I.D. : _____

Email Used : _____

Password : _____

Notes :

Notes :

Account Name: _____

Website : _____

User I.D. : _____

Email Used : _____

Password : _____

Account Name: _____

Website : _____

User I.D. : _____

Email Used : _____

Password : _____

Notes :

Don't be feeling blue

Smile

Don't be feeling blue

Password Journal

Notes :

Account Name: _____

Website : _____

User I.D. : _____

Email Used : _____

Password : _____

Account Name: _____

Website : _____

User I.D. : _____

Email Used : _____

Password : _____

Notes :

Notes :

Account Name: _____

Website : _____

User I.D. : _____

Email Used : _____

Password : _____

Account Name: _____

Website : _____

User I.D. : _____

Email Used : _____

Password : _____

Notes :

Don't be feeling blue

Smile

Don't be feeling blue

Password Journal

Notes :

Account Name: _____

Website : _____

User I.D. : _____

Email Used : _____

Password : _____

Account Name: _____

Website : _____

User I.D. : _____

Email Used : _____

Password : _____

Notes :

Notes :

Account Name: _____

Website : _____

User I.D. : _____

Email Used : _____

Password : _____

Account Name: _____

Website : _____

User I.D. : _____

Email Used : _____

Password : _____

Notes :

Don't be feeling blue

Smile

Don't be feeling blue

Password Journal

Notes :

Account Name: _____

Website : _____

User I.D. : _____

Email Used : _____

Password : _____

Account Name: _____

Website : _____

User I.D. : _____

Email Used : _____

Password : _____

Notes :

Notes :

Account Name: _____

Website : _____

User I.D. : _____

Email Used : _____

Password : _____

Account Name: _____

Website : _____

User I.D. : _____

Email Used : _____

Password : _____

Notes :

Don't be feeling blue

Smile

Don't be feeling blue

Password Journal

Notes :

Account Name: _____

Website : _____

User I.D. : _____

Email Used : _____

Password : _____

Account Name: _____

Website : _____

User I.D. : _____

Email Used : _____

Password : _____

Notes :

Notes :

Account Name: _____

Website : _____

User I.D. : _____

Email Used : _____

Password : _____

Account Name: _____

Website : _____

User I.D. : _____

Email Used : _____

Password : _____

Notes :

Don't be feeling blue

Password Journal

Notes :

Account Name: _____

Website : _____

User I.D. : _____

Email Used : _____

Password : _____

Account Name: _____

Website : _____

User I.D. : _____

Email Used : _____

Password : _____

Notes :

Notes :

Account Name: _____

Website : _____

User I.D. : _____

Email Used : _____

Password : _____

Account Name: _____

Website : _____

User I.D. : _____

Email Used : _____

Password : _____

Notes :

Don't be feeling blue

Smile

Don't be feeling blue

Password Journal

Notes :

Account Name: _____

Website : _____

User I.D. : _____

Email Used : _____

Password : _____

Account Name: _____

Website : _____

User I.D. : _____

Email Used : _____

Password : _____

Notes :

Account Name: _____

Website : _____

User I.D. : _____

Email Used : _____

Password : _____

Notes :

Account Name: _____

Website : _____

User I.D. : _____

Email Used : _____

Password : _____

Notes :

Don't be feeling blue

Don't be feeling blue

Password Journal

Notes :

Account Name: _____

Website : _____

User I.D. : _____

Email Used : _____

Password : _____

Account Name: _____

Website : _____

User I.D. : _____

Email Used : _____

Password : _____

Notes :

Notes :

Account Name: _____

Website : _____

User I.D. : _____

Email Used : _____

Password : _____

Account Name: _____

Website : _____

User I.D. : _____

Email Used : _____

Password : _____

Notes :

Don't be feeling blue

Smile

Don't be feeling blue

Password Journal

Notes :

Account Name: _____

Website : _____

User I.D. : _____

Email Used : _____

Password : _____

Account Name: _____

Website : _____

User I.D. : _____

Email Used : _____

Password : _____

Notes :

Notes :

Account Name: _____

Website : _____

User I.D. : _____

Email Used : _____

Password : _____

Account Name: _____

Website : _____

User I.D. : _____

Email Used : _____

Password : _____

Notes :

Don't be feeling blue

Password Journal

Don't be feeling blue

Smile

Password Journal

Notes :

Account Name: _____

Website : _____

User I.D. : _____

Email Used : _____

Password : _____

Account Name: _____

Website : _____

User I.D. : _____

Email Used : _____

Password : _____

Notes :

Notes :

Account Name: _____

Website : _____

User I.D. : _____

Email Used : _____

Password : _____

Account Name: _____

Website : _____

User I.D. : _____

Email Used : _____

Password : _____

Notes :

Don't be feeling blue

Password Journal

Smile

Don't be feeling blue

Password Journal

Notes :

Account Name: _____

Website : _____

User I.D. : _____

Email Used : _____

Password : _____

Account Name: _____

Website : _____

User I.D. : _____

Email Used : _____

Password : _____

Notes :

Notes :

Account Name: _____

Website : _____

User I.D. : _____

Email Used : _____

Password : _____

Account Name: _____

Website : _____

User I.D. : _____

Email Used : _____

Password : _____

Notes :

Don't be feeling blue

Don't be feeling blue

Smile

Password Journal

Notes :

Account Name: _____

Website : _____

User I.D. : _____

Email Used : _____

Password : _____

Account Name: _____

Website : _____

User I.D. : _____

Email Used : _____

Password : _____

Notes :

Notes :

Account Name: _____

Website : _____

User I.D. : _____

Email Used : _____

Password : _____

Account Name: _____

Website : _____

User I.D. : _____

Email Used : _____

Password : _____

Notes :

Don't be feeling blue

Don't be feeling blue

Password Journal

Notes :

Account Name: _____

Website : _____

User I.D. : _____

Email Used : _____

Password : _____

Account Name: _____

Website : _____

User I.D. : _____

Email Used : _____

Password : _____

Notes :

Notes :

Account Name: _____

Website : _____

User I.D. : _____

Email Used : _____

Password : _____

Account Name: _____

Website : _____

User I.D. : _____

Email Used : _____

Password : _____

Notes :

Don't be feeling blue

Smile

Don't be feeling blue

Password Journal

Notes :

Account Name: _____

Website : _____

User I.D. : _____

Email Used : _____

Password : _____

Account Name: _____

Website : _____

User I.D. : _____

Email Used : _____

Password : _____

Notes :

Notes :

Account Name: _____

Website : _____

User I.D. : _____

Email Used : _____

Password : _____

Notes :

Account Name: _____

Website : _____

User I.D. : _____

Email Used : _____

Password : _____

Notes :

Don't be feeling blue

Smile

Don't be feeling blue

Password Journal

Notes :

Account Name: _____

Website : _____

User I.D. : _____

Email Used : _____

Password : _____

Account Name: _____

Website : _____

User I.D. : _____

Email Used : _____

Password : _____

Notes :

Notes :

Account Name: _____

Website : _____

User I.D. : _____

Email Used : _____

Password : _____

Account Name: _____

Website : _____

User I.D. : _____

Email Used : _____

Password : _____

Notes :

Don't be feeling blue

Password Journal

Don't be feeling blue

Notes

www.ingramcontent.com/pod-product-compliance
Lightning Source LLC
Chambersburg PA
CBHW081334090426

42737CB00017B/3133